INTERNET Basics

An Educator's Guide

To Traveling

The Information Highway

by Dan H. Wishnietsky

Phi Delta Kappa Educational Foundation
Bloomington, Indiana
U.S.A.

Cover design by
Victoria Voelker

Phi Delta Kappa Educational Foundation
408 North Union Street
Post Office Box 789
Bloomington, Indiana 47402-0789
U.S.A.

Printed in the United States of America

Library of Congress Catalog Card Number 97-69652
ISBN 0-87367-394-8
Copyright © 1997 by Dan H. Wishnietsky
All rights reserved.

TABLE OF CONTENTS

Introduction 1

Chapter One
The On-Ramp of the Information Highway 5
    The Beginning of the Internet 6
    The Internet as a Tool for Educators 8
    Electronic Mail, or E-mail 11
    Accessing Internet Resources 15

Chapter Two
Cruising on the World Wide Web 19
    Web Browsers 20
    Using a Web Browser 22
    Internet Search Engines 27

Chapter Three
Scenic Vistas Along the Highway 29
    Locating Educational Sites 29
    Government 30
    Interactive Sites and Penpals 31
    Libraries and Reference Centers 31
    Literature and Writing 32
    Museums 33
    Science 34

Chapter Four
Other Roads, Other Places 35
    Telnet 36
    File Transfer Protocol 37
    Newsgroups 39
    Mailing Lists 41
    Accessing Additional Search Engines 42

Chapter Five
Road Maps to Curriculum Integration 45
    The Internet as a Resource Tool 46
    Student Projects Using the Internet 48
    Evaluating Internet Resources 50
    Avoiding Inappropriate Material 54

Glossary 57

INTRODUCTION

For many people, it was as if God said, "Let there be Internet," and there was Internet. Seemingly without notice or warning, this previously unknown computer network became an integral part of our worldwide culture and society. Everywhere there are references to this great electronic highway to myriad information sources that are available through personal computers. Advertisements in newspapers and on television direct readers and viewers to locations on the World Wide Web section of the Internet. During television newscasts, listeners are told about web locations that offer more details about news stories. Companies, government entities, and individuals have developed — or are developing — Internet sites to provide people with information about their products and services. Public service announcements proclaim the importance of technology and Internet access in the nation's schools. Clearly, the Information Age really has arrived.

Even before the technology was widely known, some educators believed that incorporating Internet resources into the curriculum would have a profound effect on teaching and learning. This belief by a few educators expanded into a consensus as the influence of technology and the Information Age grew. But even as most teachers agree that well-planned uses of technology are an essential part of instruction, a large number of teachers at all levels of schooling feel overwhelmed by the technology or, worse, left behind by its rapid advance. Previous changes in school technology have been modest and emerged gradually — blackboards to overhead projectors, straight pens to ballpoints, slide rules to calculators. But current computer-based technologies are different; their evolution is complex and rapid. Not surprisingly, many educators are apprehensive; they do not have adequate inservice training on the new technology, even as their schools are being equipped with the hardware and software.

An old Chinese proverb states that a journey of a thousand miles begins with the first step. This brief guide will help the uninitiated take their first steps on the information highway and become literate in the use of basic Internet technologies. I have kept the use of technical language to a minimum, and terms specific to the Internet are defined in the text or the glossary. Readers need not have any previous knowledge of the Internet. All that is needed is basic familiarity with computers, especially the point and click operation of a mouse for accessing computer applications. This publication also assumes that the reader has access to a computer that is connected to the Internet and has access to a technician or technical coordinator to handle any hardware or software problems. Programming, networking, and repairing computer-based technologies are not addressed in this work.

Reading this book should be analogous to studying a driver's handbook before the licensing exam. To obtain a driver's license, one needs to know the rules of the road. It is not necessary to know how to build or repair the car. Using the Internet successfully does not take a knowledge of computer programming; it simply requires an understanding of the rules of the road, in this case, the information highway.

This guide is organized into five chapters. Chapter 1 provides a brief history of the Internet and how its resources may be used as a meaningful educational tool. In the second chapter, the reader is introduced to the World Wide Web section of the Internet and how to access information at different web sites. Chapter 3 lists the names and locations and gives a brief description of some of the more popular World Wide Web sites used by educators. Chapter 4 introduces additional Internet topics, such as telnet, file transfer, newsgroups, and mailing lists. Finally, Chapter 5 discusses the use of Internet resources in the classroom and how to avoid content that may be considered inappropriate.

A short glossary of Internet terms is provided at the end of this guide. Terms that can be found in the glossary are italicized the first time they are used in the text. For an expanded glossary of terms, readers may wish to access the Internet Literacy Consultants Glossary of Internet Terms at **http://www.matisse.net/files/glossary.html** on the World Wide Web.

Please note that whenever an Internet site address is given, it is printed in bold type. Addresses that wrap from one line to the next are printed without a hyphen and, when used to access a site, should be typed without any spaces. Slashes and periods are specific and must be included; an address may end with a slash but *not* with a period.

My hope is that the information in this guide will take educators far enough along the information highway that they will want to travel the road often and soon will develop enough confidence to cruise in the fast lane.

CHAPTER ONE

The On-Ramp of the Information Highway

Simply stated, the Internet consists of several million computers linked together by high-speed data lines for sharing information and resources.

Consider a high school principal using the word-processing program located on his or her computer to record successful lesson plans. If the principal desires to disclose this information to the school's teachers or the district superintendent, he or she has several options. For example, the information might be printed, and that *hard copy* can be physically mailed or taken to the desired recipients. Another option is to save the information electronically in a data file on a computer disk and then to physically send each intended recipient a disk, which the recipient then could put into his or her own computer.

But a more powerful method for communicating the information can be to use computers that are connected to one another, that is, a *network*. For example, after entering the data, the principal might transmit the information from his or her computer to the computers of the teachers, the superintendent, or any other individuals who are connected to the network. Once the information has been sent to the other computers, the superintendent or the teachers can work with the information in a variety of ways: file it electronically on their own computers, update and retransmit it, respond to it, and so on, as needed. The real power of any network increases as the number of connected users grows and more information becomes available to all of those users.

The Internet is called the "network of networks," because of its enormous scope and the vast amount of information that can be obtained through the network. While networks in buildings may be physically connected by wiring, the Internet and other large networks are connected by high-speed telephone lines, using computer *modems*. Thus "on the Internet" are computers of the military services, various branches and units of government, commercial and noncommercial organizations, education institutions, and so on, that are located throughout the world. These connected computers enable educators to access information about almost any topic, collaborate with peers around the world as easily as if they were down the hall, subscribe to topical mailing lists, join discussion groups, and retrieve or send files that may incorporate pictures, sounds, and video clips as well as traditional text.

The Beginning of the Internet

The genesis of the Internet can be found within the diverse elements of what has been characterized as the military-industrial complex. In 1956, after the U.S.S.R. launched Sputnik, the United States established the Advanced Research Projects Agency (ARPA) within the Department of Defense (DOD) to help strengthen science and technology. One of the proposals suggested by ARPA was the formation of a computer-based communication network that would enable all types of computers to communicate with each other using a common language. In 1969 the beginnings of this type of network became a reality. To expedite communication among its researchers, the Department of Defense funded a project that linked DOD computers and computers located at universities working on military projects. The emerging network, called ARPANET (Advanced Research Projects Administration Network) began in 1969 with only three computers connected by telephone lines. By 1984 the number of computers on ARPANET was more than a thousand.

As more and more universities and research institutions connected, the data lines became so crowded that many people started to get the equivalent of a busy signal whenever they tried to transmit data. To satisfy this burgeoning demand for both military and education applications, ARPANET was divided into several channels for different uses. These channels were linked according to a set of rules that computers use to send information from one computer to another. Called the Transmission Control Protocol and Internet Protocol (TCP/IP), these rules enabled the increasing number of users to continue exchanging information within the growing network. The protocols also helped to define the Internet as a connected set of computers using TCP/IP.

During the 1980s a major change occurred in computing. Many university applications that required a large mainframe computer could now be performed on a desktop computer. Computing power moved from the mainframe in the locked room to the faculty office and the student lab. By connecting these desktop computers to a computer on ARPANET, all members of the university community gained access to the network resources, not just the high-level researchers. And so it should not be surprising that by the late 1980s ARPANET had more data transmission than it could manage.

To handle, again, the increasing number of users, the National Science Foundation in 1986 established NSFNet, a larger and more powerful computer network than ARPANET; and in 1990 ARPANET was discontinued for lack of use. The NSFNet continued to grow as desktop computers became less expensive and connecting to the network became easier. Within a short period, the Internet data lines of NSFNet were joined with data lines of major telecommunication companies, such as AT&T, WorldCom, Sprint, MCI, and the Bell telephone companies; and the modern Internet was born.

Now, any person with a computer, modem, and a phone line is able to connect to the Internet by subscribing to a commercial on-line service or an Internet service provider. The first K-12 schools were connected to the Internet in 1988, and by 1994 more than a thousand secondary schools were online. By the year 2000, it is expected that most educators will have access to Internet resources through their school's computer or through a computer and modem in their home.

Recognizing that technology was becoming an important part of society, the United States Congress passed and President Bush signed the High-Performance Computing Act of 1991. One purpose of this bill was to create a federal program that would establish a National Research and Education Network (NREN). NREN would be a high-speed, high-capacity data network that would ensure that all users would be able to transmit and receive data quickly and easily. This became especially important in 1992 as World Wide Web (WWW) technology became part of the Internet. Instead of just sending and receiving text, users of the Internet now could route graphics, audio, and video. Students, educators, and others would be able to readily access and retrieve online information located in libraries, museums, research facilities, organizations, government agencies, and many other important databases located throughout the world.

The Internet as a Tool for Educators

The Internet is just one of many tools for educators to use. As chalk, the overhead projector, calculators, and manipulatives are tools, so is the Internet. The primary test for any tool occurs when teachers decide if they can teach better with the tool than without it and if learning increases when the tool is employed. A feature of the Internet that helps improve teaching and learning is its inexpensive and instant communication capability. Called electronic mail, or *e-mail*, this feature enables any person on the Internet to communicate electronically with any other person on the Internet.

For example, science teachers in different countries have communicated through the Internet and designed a project in which students compare the number of daylight hours on specific dates at their location. Using the Internet, their students electronically sent each other the required information, such as the number of minutes of daylight for each date and the longitude and latitude of their location. After the data were exchanged, each class formed a conclusion; and then the students exchanged their thoughts through the electronic network. The students benefited by collecting and using actual data, collaborating with students from other cultures, and communicating their conclusions with each other.

Another feature of the Internet is its ability to quickly access an almost infinite number of resources. One perpetual complaint concerning traditional textbooks is that even if they were copyrighted this year, the information often is two or more years old. This is especially problematic when the textbook nears the end of the adoption cycle and may be eight or ten years old. For example, an eighth-grade text may talk about the Soviet Union as if it was still intact; and while the eighth-grade teachers may not be able to buy new textbooks, they can use Internet resources to give the students a current map of Eastern Europe and information about the states of the former U.S.S.R.

Teachers also can use Internet resources to provide students with the information as it is occurring. When the Hubble Telescope was sending pictures to NASA, the pictures were available through the Internet within days of being received. The pictures were not there only for researchers, but were made available to students and teachers with an Internet connection. Similar examples can be found in every discipline. The resources of the information highway are invaluable as a way to ensure that students are presented with the most current available information.

Educators usually are connected to the Internet through their school network, an online service, or an Internet service provider. An increasing number of schools are connecting directly to a *host* computer on the Internet through a high-speed data line. The teacher activates the computer hardware on his or her desk and follows the required protocol, or steps, to connect. This procedure usually consists of typing one command or clicking on an *icon*, or small graphic, on the computer screen and then entering a personal *password* (a unique combination of letters and numbers that prevents someone else from using the same account). A negative aspect of direct access is that teachers typically have to be at school to access their account. To solve this problem, the school's host computer may allow telephone access. The teacher can connect to the host computer from any other computer by using a modem, phone line, and communication software. If telephone access to their school network is not available, many educators personally subscribe to an online or Internet service.

When teachers are accessing an Internet account through an online service or Internet service provider, such as America Online or AT&T, the desktop computer connects to the host computer using a modem and a phone line. The service provides the required telecommunication software to connect to their service. Teachers, or the school's computer technician, simply install the software onto their computer by following the included directions. In most cases, the user has to enter only two or three commands. The computer dials the host computer's phone number, and the teacher enters the correct password to be connected. A negative aspect of using the phone line is that it requires more time to access and receive information than when the user has a direct connection. (Modems can be purchased in several different speeds. When a phone connection is used, the minimum recommended modem speed is 28.8, or 28,800 bits per second.)

The influence of technology in our culture has almost mandated that computers and Internet resources be a part of every school's curriculum. Most people with a computer, a modem, and a phone line can access Internet resources for less than $20 per month. Because computers and their related technologies are becoming an integral part of society, people who are not technology literate soon may be at the same disadvantage as individuals who are not able to read and write. Even the neighborhood bowling alley is using computer technology to score games and calculate standings and averages. All students need to have access to technology through the school and be taught how it should be used and controlled.

Electronic Mail, or E-mail

An electronic mail system is an Internet application that electronically transmits, stores, and delivers written messages. Electronic mail, or e-mail, was developed because of the limitations of other delivery systems, such as the postal system and the telephone. When compared to electronic mail, the postal service is slow and sometimes not dependable. The problem with the telephone is that it is not effective unless the person called can be located; and even when the person can be found, he or she may be unable to accept the call at that time. And, of course, the telephone produces no written record.

Electronic mail overcomes "mailroom drag" and "telephone tag" by its speed and its ability to store written messages. When an educator establishes an Internet account, he or she is assigned a unique Internet address. Anyone with access to the Internet who knows the person's e-mail address can send that person a message electronically. And anyone who can receive e-mail also can send it. Usually Internet provider host computers are online at all times, allowing electronic mail to be sent and received 24 hours a day.

For example, suppose Dr. Smith, a school superintendent, has an Internet account and wishes to send a message to Dr. Clark, a professor of education at a university in another state who also has an e-mail address. Dr. Smith accesses her computer's Internet electronic mail application and types a message. Without leaving her desk, she instructs her computer to send Dr. Clark the message through the Internet. Usually within a few minutes, the message "arrives" and is stored in the computer's electronic mailboxes for future retrieval. If Dr. Clark is using his computer when the message arrives, his computer notifies him that he has new mail stored in his mailbox. When it is convenient, Dr. Clark reads the message and responds appropriately. If Dr. Clark is teaching when the e-mail arrives, the host computer stores the message and notifies him of its arrival the next time he uses his computer. He then retrieves it at his convenience.

An Internet address has three parts: the *username*, the *domain name*, and the *top-domain name*. The username is the name of the person or organization, or the account name, at the Internet address. The domain name in the address is the name of the host computer (or service provider) where the account is located. And the top-domain name indicates the type of location the host computer represents. Some top-domain names include "gov" for government, "com" for a commercial service, "edu" for an education organization, "mil" for the military, and "org" for organizations that are not categorized by another top-domain name. For example, to send an e-mail message to the President of the United States, a user would enter the address as **president@whitehouse.gov**. (There is no period after the address itself.) "President" is the username; "whitehouse" is the domain name; "gov" is the top-domain name, an abbreviation of government.

In addition to top-domain abbreviations, there are two-letter country code abbreviations for host computers located outside the United States. The United States country code, "us", is optional. If a person wants to send e-mail to John Smith at the Australian

Capital Territory Education Information Network in Canberra, Australia, for example, the address would be written as **jsmith@ freenet.actein.edu.au**, with the "au" designating Australia. Note in this example that the address uses multiple domain names; the names following the @ sign are separated by periods (called "dots" in computer language). Internet addresses cannot contain spaces; therefore, words usually are run together or separated by dots.

To write and send an e-mail message, the Internet user must access the mail software application on his or her computer. There are many mail programs, but most are similar in operation. The description that follows is based on a mail application that uses command buttons, icons, or pictures that, when "clicked" (activated by using the mouse's point-and-click function), will execute appropriate functions for sending mail. Following are typical steps:

1. After entering the mail application, move the arrow to the "send mail" or "new mail" button and click. The monitor will display a mail screen that has at least three sections: to, subject, and message.
2. The "to" section is where the Internet address of the intended recipient must be typed. Enter that address.
3. The "subject" section will display a short description of what the message is about. Enter that description.
4. The "message" section is the main text area. Type the message. If the message is extremely long, it may be easier to compose it in a word-processing program, save it as a separate electronic file, and then attach it to a shorter e-mail message.
5. When the message is ready to be sent, use the mouse to move the cursor to click the "send" button; and in a few seconds the message will be traveling through the Internet data lines to its destination.

Other features found on most Internet mail programs include the ability to send the same e-mail message to more than one person at a time, to attach a file to an electronic mail message, and to establish an address book to record frequently used Internet addresses. For example, suppose a teacher is in a graduate program and is writing her thesis. She enters her e-mail address book and types the names of her committee members with their e-mail addresses. Then, instead of trying to remember all of the e-mail addresses and typing in each one separately every time she wants to communicate with the committee, the teacher simply can open her electronic address book and click the desired address or group of addresses; they will be automatically placed in the "to" section of the mail screen. If draft chapters from the thesis need to be sent, the teacher clicks the "attach file" icon; and the mail program will prompt the teacher to write the name of the file that is to be sent. The program then will locate the named, stored file and transmit it with the message.

When accessing an Internet account, the computer indicates if there is new mail in the user's mailbox. This can be with an icon, a sound clip, or both. The icon usually is an envelope, and the sound clip has the computer state that new mail has arrived. (On AOL, for example, a voice announces, "You've got mail!") The user then may use the mouse to click the mail icon and enter the mail program. A listing of new mail messages appears on the screen, usually consisting of the name of the sender and the subject line. To read the e-mail, the user will click the icon corresponding to the desired message and the message appears on the screen.

Once the message is read, the user has several options regarding the e-mail. One is to save the information on the computer's hard drive for future use. This is accomplished by clicking the "save" icon and naming the file. Another is to produce a hard copy by clicking the "print" icon. If the computer does not have a printer, the message can be stored on a disk as a text file and moved to a computer with a word processor and a printer. The word processor reads the text file and prints it. A stored text file also can be edited and used in other word-processing documents.

An e-mail message also can be forwarded to other people on the Internet by clicking the "forward" icon and typing in the e-mail address of the person who is to receive the forwarded message. For example, when a teacher receives an e-mail with information that is worth sharing with colleagues, he or she can pass it on easily by simply clicking a few buttons.

If the person receiving the message wishes to answer the sender, he or she clicks the "reply" button. The previously described mail screen will appear; however, in the "to" and "subject" sections there will be the address of the sender and the subject of the received message. The reply is written in the "message" section of the screen, and the "send" icon is clicked. Then the reply is on its way.

Accessing Internet Resources

In addition to sending messages, educators can use the Internet to access information that is available on thousands of host computers. Companies, organizations, education institutions, governments, and other groups have compiled and stored information on their computers in a format that enables computer users with Internet accounts to have access to the information. Some examples: Automobile companies provide information about their cars; Canada presents data about its provinces and cities; and the library at the University of Texas at Austin has country and city maps from every part of the world. Individuals with Internet accounts soon discover that audio, video, graphic, and text data are readily available for almost every conceivable subject.

To access the resources available on the Internet, educators can use any of several communication programs for accessing the host computers on which the information is located. These communication programs, or *browsers*, enable the user to connect to the host computers and to obtain information; the method is similar to that used by the e-mail communication software. When sending electronic mail, the address is an individual person with an account on a specific host computer. When searching for information on the World Wide Web or other network, the address is a file of information located on a particular host computer. For example, information about congressional legislation is located on the host computer, **thomas.loc.gov**. This location address indicates that the file is located on a computer named "thomas" at the Library of Congress ("loc"), which is a government agency ("gov"). A personal name before an @ sign in the address is not required because only the host computer is being notified, not an individual. If a teacher or student desired the full text of the *Congressional Record*, he or she would use the browsing tool to contact "thomas" and request the appropriate database of information. The host computer would then send the solicited data through Internet data lines to the computer of the student who made the request.

One example of a browser is *Gopher*, which is used to connect to information stored on Internet computers called Gopher servers. Most commercial online services and Internet service providers have Gopher access. Usually an icon is labeled "Gopher," or the word "Gopher" is part of a name. After clicking the icon and connecting to a Gopher server, a main menu will appear on the screen to list folders of information sorted by topics. By using the arrow keys or, in some systems, by clicking the mouse, different topics on the menu can be highlighted. Pressing the return key or clicking the mouse opens the highlighted menu item to reveal another menu of information. Topics on each succeeding menu can be opened in similar fashion until the desired information is obtained.

For example, a student connected to the Gopher site of the United States House of Representatives will view a menu that includes House e-mail addresses, House leadership information, educational resources, House schedules, and many other topics. If the student desires to send a member of Congress a message by electronic mail, he or she can highlight the menu item, "House E-mail Addresses," and view a list of House members and their corresponding e-mail addresses. After obtaining the desired information, the student can save the file and return to the original menu by typing the applicable commands or clicking the appropriate icons, depending on the features of the system. The student then enters the e-mail program, types the address in the "to" section of the screen, and sends the e-mail message.

Often, it is enjoyable just to browse, or "surf," the Internet by exploring the Gopher menus for information. However, if a teacher or a student requires data about a specific topic, surfing the Internet is not an efficient method for finding the information. Information stored at Gopher servers may be located quickly and easily by using a search tool, or *search engine*, called Veronica. When accessing the main menu of a Gopher server, one menu item usually is a folder or icon with the word "search" in it. Opening that folder will reveal a menu of Veronica sites for finding Gopher directories by title or by a *keyword*. After highlighting the menu item and pressing the return key, the Veronica "Find what?" dialog box will appear. Type one or more keywords in the dialog box and press return, and Veronica will search Gopher services worldwide to find directories that match the keywords. These directories are listed in a temporary Gopher menu based on the search. This menu may be browsed and the directories accessed as with a permanent Gopher menu.

To (electronically) remember site locations and avoid having to search again, most Gopher programs have a "bookmark" feature. The name of an important location or its icon may be copied into the bookmark file. It then becomes part of the bookmark menu that is saved on the user's computer. To access a bookmarked site, the user merely opens the bookmark folder, highlights the site name, and presses return. The Gopher program then searches the Internet and opens the chosen location. When the user no longer wishes to have the site bookmarked, it can be deleted easily.

CHAPTER TWO

Cruising on the World Wide Web

The World Wide Web is the superhighway of the Internet. Instead of using a Gopher-style hierarchy of menus to access information, which was described in Chapter One, the World Wide Web uses text and graphics to link resources around the world.

In 1965 Ted Nelson, a student at Harvard University, began work on a system that would logically link material from one class (or form) of communication with material from other classes. He called his system *hypertext*, a term defined as non-sequential writing. Nelson conceived of a computer system in which text would be displayed on an interactive screen that provided users with the option of branching to other appropriate texts. In 1968 a hypertext system developed by Nelson and Andries van Dam was used to link documents for the Apollo moon missions. Another hypertext system, developed in 1968 by Douglas Engelbart, was used at the Stanford Research Institute to link computer files.

In 1992 the European Laboratory for Particle Physics developed and introduced a *hypermedia* system known as the World Wide Web (WWW), or simply the Web, to link Internet resources. The World Wide Web is a hypermedia system because it uses computer hardware and software to link many forms of data, such as pictures, sounds, and video, in addition to text. Each document, or page, of stored information on the World Wide Web is linked by paths. Unlike the menu system used by Gopher servers, there is no set path that users have to travel. The order in which a person explores the World Wide Web is determined by interest, experience, and need. To guide users among the documents, web pages include on-screen "hot spots," or "hot links," that connect that page of information with other documents. These hot spots may be text, icons, drawings, or any other part of the computer screen that is linked to other documents. When the cursor is moved to one of these hot spots and the mouse is clicked, the requested information is displayed.

Web Browsers

At present the World Wide Web is the fastest growing portion of the Internet and the section most often used by teachers to find education resources. To access the Web, educators need a graphical browser, such as Netscape Navigator, Internet Explorer, or Mosaic. A graphical browser is essential in order to display both the graphics and text portions of the web page on the computer screen.

Graphical browsers are built into computer networks by the system operators, and various service providers use various browsers. To access the browser, the user clicks on the browser icon on the computer screen. The computer "launches," or activates, the browser, which establishes an Internet connection and connects the user to the browser's *home page*. The home page is the document that the browser is programmed to find first. This could be the "Welcome to Netscape" document, for example.

From this home page, the browser will find other home pages — other first pages of web sites — such as the school's own home page if one has been developed or the home page of a museum or a company, including an online bookstore.

The browser is able to locate and retrieve web pages by using a Universal Resource Locator, or URL. The URL is an Internet resource address that specifies a document's location on the Internet. It contains at least two and sometimes three essential pieces of information: **HOW://WHERE/WHAT**. The "HOW" and "WHERE" part of the address are always required.

The "HOW" refers to the protocol, or set of rules, used to retrieve the resource. For example, when the resource is a World Wide Web document, the protocol is *http*, which stands for Hypertext Transfer Protocol. Every Web address begins with this abbreviation followed by a colon and two slashes: **http://**. The address of the "Welcome to Netscape" document, for example, is **http://home.netscape.com/**. Note that there are no blank spaces in the URL, and every symbol counts. Be aware that the address does not end in a period. However, it may end in a slash, as shown here.

The **home.netscape.com** part of the address is the "WHERE." It is the domain name of the computer server that I described in the e-mail section of the previous chapter.

The "WHAT" section of the address tells the server what resource is to be retrieved. If this section is not specified, which is the case in the "Welcome to Netscape" document, a *default* document specified by the location's file server is displayed. Other resources available on the server often are linked to the default document and can be accessed by clicking highlighted "hot spots," words or pictures.

An example of a World Wide Web address with HOW://WHERE/WHAT sections is **http://gs213.sp.cs.cmu.edu/prog/dist/**. The "HOW" is **http://** and the "WHERE" is **gs213.sp.cs.cmu.edu**. The specific resource that the user desires to retrieve is the "WHAT" section of the address, in this case, **prog/dist/**. When a user activates this URL, the browser will retrieve a program that calculates distance. In this program the computer will display an interactive screen that a student or other user can use to enter two locations on the earth. The program then will calculate the distance between the two points.

Graphical browsers, such as Netscape Navigator, Internet Explorer, and Mosaic, are not limited to accessing web sites using the Hypertext Transfer Protocol. By entering the names of different protocols in the "HOW" part of the URL, the browser can access almost any resource available on the Internet. If the user desires to access a Gopher site, for example, he or she types **gopher://** in the "HOW" section before the address of the specific Gopher site. For example, the URL to access the Gopher server of the National Aeronautics and Space Administration (NASA) at the Marshall Space Flight Center, is **gopher://spacelink.msfc.nasa.gov**. The graphical browser also can access Veronica for searching gopher sites. The URL for searching gopherspace and Gopher directories is **gopher://liberty.uc.wlu.edu:70/11/gophers/veronica/**. Other protocols include **ftp://** for *file transfer protocol*, **telnet://** for a *telnet* session, and **news:** for *newsgroups*. Notice that the two slashes are not used after **news:** when accessing newsgroups.

The file transfer protocol enables Internet users to transfer files from a remote server to the hard drive of their home computer. Newsgroups are the topic discussion groups of the Internet where anyone with access can read bulletins regarding the group's topic and respond with their own postings. Using the telnet protocol, the user is able to log onto a remote computer and use that computer's resources.

Using a Web Browser

The various features of the Internet browser enable the user to find and explore Internet resources in a quick and efficient manner. After clicking the browser icon and accessing the browser home page, the user will find a menu bar and, below it, a toolbar ready to access the various features that make it possible to explore the Internet and locate needed resources. (Note: The features and procedures described in this section are based on the Netscape browser, but other browsers have similar features and incorporate equivalent commands.)

Across the top of the computer screen the menu bar will be displayed. This row of buttons will be used to pull down the various menus. A typical menu bar will contain some or all of the following:

FILE EDIT VIEW GO BOOKMARKS OPTIONS DIRECTORY HELP

To access a command in a pull-down menu, use the mouse to move the cursor to the appropriate title. The cursor will become an arrow. Press and hold the mouse button and move down the pull-down menu until the desired command is highlighted. When the mouse button is released, the highlighted command will execute. For example, the pull-down menu commands for the File menu include such options as "Open Location," "Print," and "Exit." The "Open Location" command is used when the URL of the desired location is known. If a user wants to browse the list of books published by Phi Delta Kappa International, for instance, and knows the organization's World Wide Web address, he or she can highlight "Open Location," type **http://www.pdkintl.org** in the location box, and press the return key. The browser contacts the Phi Delta Kappa International file server for the information and the PDK home page appears on the screen.

That home page, or any page of information, may be printed by using the "Print" command from the File menu. When the user finishes with the information, he or she can exit the browser by highlighting the "Exit" command.

Other commands of use to beginning Internet users are found under the View, Go, Bookmarks, and Options menu titles. For example, under View the "Reload" command can be used if the information was not properly transmitted from the file server to the user's computer. The commands of the Go menu — "Back," "Forward," and "Home" — enable the user to revisit the previous page of information and then return. The "Back" and "Forward" commands may be activated more than once in succession. If there is not a previous or forward page, the menu button will be dimmed, indicating that it cannot be used. The "Home" command may be activated at any time during an Internet session to return to the browser home page.

Also in the Go menu is the "Stop Loading" command. This command can be used when there is a problem accessing an Internet site. If a requested file server is busy with other connections or temporarily shut down, the browser may try to connect for an extended length of time. The animation of the Netscape initial, for example, is located below the toolbar and indicates that the Netscape browser is attempting to connect to the file server and transfer information. Clicking the "Stop Loading" command will stop the attempt at the transfer, which can save the user time and frustration.

Quick access to previously visited pages also can be accomplished by using the Go and Bookmarks menus. The names of sites visited during the current Internet session are automatically added to the Go menu. When a user wishes to return to a previous site visited during the same session online, he or she can activate the Go menu and highlight the desired location. The browser then will reconnect to the requested site. However, these locations are not saved once the user exits the browser program.

Saving locations for future Internet sessions requires use of the "Add Bookmarks" command in the Bookmarks menu. When viewing a page that will be useful at a later time, instead of trying to remember the address or writing the address on a slip of paper, the user can highlight the "Add Bookmarks" command, and the browser will add the location to a bookmark file. The name of the location remains in the Bookmarks menu until removed by the user. To access the site in a future session, the user simply highlights the location name under Bookmarks, and the browser retrieves the information. To remove a location from the Bookmarks menu, highlight the "Go to Bookmarks" command in the Bookmarks menu. When the browser displays the bookmarks file, simply select and highlight the location to be removed and use the delete command under the Edit menu to erase it.

Commands in the Options menu allow the user to customize how the computer screen will look when using the browser. For beginning users, the browser should display the toolbar, location, and directory buttons and should automatically load images. To verify these options, the user can highlight the Options menu and note whether there is a check mark beside the "Show Toolbar," "Show Location," "Show Directory Buttons," and "Auto Load Images." If a check mark is missing, highlight the command with the mouse and release. The command will activate and a check mark will appear. To deactivate, repeat the operation.

Below the menu bar is the toolbar with several buttons, such as "Back," "Forward," "Home," "Reload," "Images," "Open," "Find," and "Stop." These buttons activate commands that also can be found in the pull-down menus but are placed on the toolbar because they are the most commonly used commands when navigating the Internet. For example, if a teacher is searching web pages for information and decides to return to the previous page, instead of using the "Back" command in the Go pull-down menu, he or she can simply click the icon labeled "Back" to view the previous page. The other commands also are the same as found in the pull-down menus. The exception is the "Images" command, which is used when the "Auto Load Images" menu command is not checked. When images are not automatically loaded, clicking the Images command will indicate to the browser that the images should be loaded onto the current page.

Located below the toolbar is the location box. Inside the location box is the URL of the page currently displayed. The location box may be used in place of the "Open Location" command in the File menu. Use the mouse to move the cursor inside the location field and click. Highlight the current URL by dragging the mouse, as in any word-processor program, then type in the URL of the desired location and press return. The browser will search for the site of the new URL and retrieve the information.

Corresponding with the URL is the title of the displayed page. The page title is not part of the URL. Rather, it is the name of the page as designated by the page's author. The page title is displayed in a window title bar located at the top center of the screen. For example, when searching the ERIC database on the World Wide Web, the URL in the location box will be **http://ericir.syr.edu/eric/eric.html**, and the title, "ERIC Query Form," will appear in the title bar. The page title also will be displayed in the Go and Bookmarks menus; however, when that page title is highlighted in those menus, it is the corresponding URL that the browser uses to connect to the requested location.

Directory buttons, found below the location box, provide useful information for users who are learning how to navigate the Internet. Using the mouse to click the "What's New" and "What's Cool" buttons will display information about new and interesting (presumably "cool") Internet sites. For example, if the user clicks "What's Cool," a list of "cool" page names and a short description of each page's content will appear. The user then can highlight a page name, and the browser will find the page and display it. Each of the "cool" pages also contains highlighted words that link to other web pages.

Below the directory buttons is the large display of the web page. To view the different sections of the page, the user can click the arrows on the vertical and horizontal scroll bars. This will move the screen in the direction of the arrow. If a word or phrase on the page is highlighted in color (and underlined for identification on black-and-white monitors), that text is a "hot link" to another web page, in the same way that such links are used in the "What's Cool" page and other areas.

By using the browser, the student or teacher can explore numerous byways along the information highway. Whenever the path comes to an apparent dead end, the user can easily back out (using the "Back" button) or head for home — the home page, that is — by using the "Home" button.

Internet Search Engines

Often it is enjoyable and informative simply to browse the Internet, rather like taking a Sunday drive along the information highway. The diversity of topics to be found is truly amazing. However, such browsing is not an efficient way to find data about particular topics. To bypass irrelevant home pages and quickly locate desired information, the World Wide Web employs software programs called search engines. Search engines are software programs that scan the Internet for web pages with details about specific topics.

To activate a search engine, one way is to click the "Net Search" directory button, which will display a list of Internet search engines. Next, click one of the highlighted search engine names. The browser will display the requested search engine home page on the screen.

Once the search engine home page is displayed, the user can type a keyword or phrase in the search box and press the return key. The search engine will scan the Internet and return a list of sites and site summaries that match the keyword(s) entered. After reading the site summaries, the user can highlight and click a site name, and that site's home page will be accessed. If that site proves unhelpful or another site is needed, then the user can click the "Back" key to return to the list and choose another site.

For individuals familiar with ERIC searches, searching the Internet using a search engine is similar to undertaking an ERIC database search using the keyword option. When searching the ERIC database, the user types one or more keywords connected by relation operators (such as AND or OR) to narrow or expand the query. In similar fashion, the Internet user types one or more keywords and relation operators onto the search engine's home page to initiate a search. The procedures vary slightly among search engines; however, specific instructions for conducting a search usually are located on the search engine's home page.

Three well-known search engines listed on the Net Search page are Yahoo, Alta Vista, and Infoseek. Yahoo was developed in 1994 by two graduate students whose goal was to help organize the Internet. Staffers at Yahoo have visited and categorized more than 370,000 web sites. This growing number of sites organized by the Yahoo staffers is only a small part of the World Wide Web, but it is a useful place to start searching. The Yahoo home page also contains links to sports scores, weather, news headlines, stock quotes, and other search engines.

Alta Vista and Infoseek search many more pages than Yahoo. This can be both a blessing and a curse. For example, when I typed "CDs and rates" to find current rates for bank certificates of deposit, Yahoo listed about 12 sites, while Alta Vista and Infoseek itemized about 500,000 locations. But most of those 500,000 sites are not about the bank CDs. They are about music CDs — compact discs.

With the powerful search engines, it is important to plan the keyword search carefully to prevent receiving a long, useless list. Fortunately, both Alta Vista and Infoseek do contain site summaries to help the user decide which site names to click and search in order to find the needed information.

CHAPTER THREE

Scenic Vistas Along the Highway

This chapter is devoted to finding a few of the many educational sites — I dub them the "scenic vistas" — on the information highway. Of course, there are hundreds of useful sites for educators on the World Wide Web. Frequently at meetings and conferences, educators who use the Internet spend time updating each other about new sites that they have found. This chapter can present only a short introductory list of such locations, but these home pages should be a helpful beginning for educators' Internet journeys.

Locating Educational Sites

Readers should keep in mind that the information highway has a life of its own and the World Wide Web is dynamic and ever-changing. Although I expect the sites listed in this chapter to continue to be maintained — and to have the same URL — there are no guarantees. Thus, if the site is not accessible at the URL given, it would be wise to initiate a search using one of the search engines discussed in Chapter 2, as the site may still exist at a different location.

For each site I have included the site name, the URL, and a brief description. The URL is printed in bold and should be typed in the location box of the Internet browser exactly as written here. *Remember not to put in any spaces, and do not put a period at the end of the address.* Also, note that some sites have multiple purposes. I have placed SunSite Reference Server in the science section, for example, because it has links to a weather server; but it also includes government hypertexts, archives, and other links. It is often the case on the information highway, as along any highway, that one scenic vista may open on another and yet another. Traveling through the electronic links can be like driving down a byway; sometimes it proves useful and other times it turns out to be a dead end.

Government

CIA Publications and Handbooks
http://www.odci.gov/cia/publications/pubs.html
This site provides students and teachers with information about countries, international organizations, and international agreements. There also is a section with reference maps.

U.S. Department of Education
http://www.ed.gov/
The Department of Education homepage contains information about grants, guides for teachers and students, publications and products, and major initiatives in education. There also are links to other educational resources available on the Internet.

The White House
http://www.whitehouse.gov
The White House web site provides information about the President and Vice President, a tour of the White House, an interactive

citizens' handbook, a virtual library of White House documents, and a special section for young people.

Supreme Court Decisions
http://www.law.cornell.edu/lii.table.html

The Cornell Law School and Legal Information Institute provides the full text of U.S. Supreme Court decisions, the U.S. Code, and the *Cornell Law Review*.

U.S. Congress
http://thomas.loc.gov

The Thomas Legislative Information site is published by the Library of Congress and includes congressional documents, bill summaries, bill texts, bill status, and the *Congressional Record*. Also available at this location is information concerning the legislative process and such legislative branch Internet sites as the House, Senate, Library of Congress, Government Printing Office, and Government Accounting Office.

Interactive Sites and Penpals

Global Networking for Students
http://www.kidlink.org

The KIDLINK home page presents a dialogue project that attempts to involve students between 10 and 15 years of age in global discussion. Since 1990 more than 60,000 young people from 87 countries have participated.

Libraries and Reference Centers

Kids Web WWW Digital Library
http://www.npac.syr.edu/textbook/kidsweb/

This site provides links to computers worldwide and is searchable by general areas of the arts, the sciences, social studies, and other disciplines. This site is part of the Living Textbook Project from the Northeast Parallel Architectures Center at Syracuse University.

AskERIC
http://ericir.syr.edu
The Educational Resources Information Center (ERIC) provides services for teachers, library media specialists, administrators, and others. Submit a request for information related to education and receive an answer within 48 hours from the AskERIC staff. The AskERIC staff will search ERIC databases, *ERIC Digests*, and Internet resources; or users may conduct their own ERIC database search. This site also houses a "Virtual Library" consisting of lesson plans, special projects, television series companion materials, and other education-related materials.

Public Libraries
http://sjcpl.lib.in.us/homepage/publiclibraries/publiclibraryservers.html
The St. Joseph County Public Library site contains a list, with links, of public libraries with Internet services.

Quick Reference
http://www.lib.utexas.edu/libs/pcl/reference.html
This reference server lists and links the user to more than a hundred references available on the Internet. Listed are links to major reference works; English language, other language, and topical dictionaries; newspapers; electronic books and journals; research databases; and telephone and e-mail directories. There also are links to other reference servers.

Literature and Writing

Shakespeare on the Internet
http://www.shakespeare.com/
This site provides discussion groups, links to current production schedules for Shakespeare companies and festivals, and links to web sites where users may search the complete works of Shakespeare.

Online Writing Lab
http://owl.trc.purdue.edu/

This site, sponsored by Purdue University, presents information about topics related to writing and links to other writing sites.

Museums

Smithsonian Institution
http://www.si.edu

This site provides links to the museums and organizations that are part of the Smithsonian Institution. There also are links to Smithsonian events, activities, resources, and tours.

Franklin Institute Service Museum
http://sln.fi.edu

The Franklin Institute Service museum in Philadelphia offers online exhibits that support science curricula. Examples include study units on the heart, the experiments of Ben Franklin, and a guide to the universe. This site also contains links to educational hot spots on the Internet. Below is a partial list of the URLs by discipline for educators who desire direct access to the resource pages. A complete list of disciplines is available on the Franklin Institute home page.

American History and Government Hotlist
http://sln.fi.edu/tfi/hotlists/government.html

Geography Hotlist
http://sln.fi.edu/tfi/hotlists/geography.html

Literature Hotlist
http://sln.fi.edu/tfi/hotlists/literature.html

Mathematics Hotlist
http://sln.fi.edu/tfi/hotlists/math.html

The Reference Hotlist
http://sln.fi.edu/tfi/hotlists/reference.html

Science

Exploratorium ExploraNet
http://www.exploratorium.edu
This site includes electronic exhibits, news, and resources for teachers and students. There also is a digital library of exhibits, still images, and sounds. The location is published by the Palace of Fine Arts in San Francisco.

The Nine Planets
http://seds.lpl.arizona.edu/nineplanets/nineplanets/nineplanets.html
This multimedia tour of the solar system is published by the University of Arizona Chapter of Students for the Exploration and Development of Space. Each of the planets and its major moons is described with text, pictures, sounds, and video clips.

SunSITE Reference Server
http://sunsite.unc.edu
SunSITE at the University of North Carolina provides links to a weather server, government hypertexts, education archives, and various multimedia exhibits.

NASA Online
http://www.nasa.gov
The National Aeronautics and Space Administration site provides information about human space flight, aeronautics research, technology development, and space science. There is a gallery of still images, video clips, and audio clips that can be downloaded and there are links to related web locations.

CHAPTER FOUR

Other Roads, Other Places

Any great highway has byways and lesser traveled paths, and the Internet is no exception. Other functions of the Internet that will be helpful to educators and their students include telnet, file transfers, newsgroups, and mailing lists.

Telnet, which I mentioned previously, is a protocol that enables a user to log onto other host computers on the Internet and to use the remote computer's resources. File transfer is another Internet protocol. It uses file transfer protocol (FTP) programs, and so students and teachers are able to transfer files of data between Internet host computers and the local classroom computer. These files may include text, pictures, sounds, or video clips.

Newsgroups and mailing lists are two ways in which people on the Internet can have discussions about topics that interest them. Newsgroups are electronic, topic-centered bulletin boards, where users may read other peoples' comments on a topic and then post their own ideas. Mailing lists are similar to newsgroups, except that the user must "subscribe," or register with, the electronic mail forum on the topic of interest; and the discussion is accomplished through electronic mail.

Telnet

The telnet protocol enables students and teachers in one location to access and use the resources available on other Internet host computers. For example, a teacher who is registered in a graduate program at a university located in a distant city may need to use the statistics program located on that school's computer. The first thought might be to drive to the campus computer center and perform the required work. However, if the university's computer allows Internet access, a telnet program will eliminate the need to travel. Instead of driving to the campus, the teacher can telnet to the university computer through the Internet, *login*, and use the statistics package. The local computer will imitate a terminal on the host computer.

Other telnet uses include accessing libraries, registering for classes, and accessing other databases for research purposes. In some cases, the user must have an assigned login (an account name) and a password to access the resources. However, many sites allow public access to their location.

One such site that allows public access is located at the Dartmouth College Library. Resources include a World Factbook, the full text of Shakespeare's plays, the King James Bible, and many other online services. To access this location, the user can open the Internet browser, click the "Open" button on the tool bar, and type the following URL: **telnet://library.dartmouth.edu**. The browser will access the Dartmouth College Library Online System and the first page of information will appear on the computer screen. This page supplies necessary information on login and logoff, instructions for navigating through the databases, and the escape character in case there is a problem with the telnet session. The Dartmouth location does not require a login sequence; however, the user must type "select file" for a menu of available information. The user should carefully read the instructions on the screen and type "bye" to end the telnet session. If the host computer requests the terminal type, usually in the form, "Term = ", the user should type "vt100."

Two other telnet sites of interest to educators are the geography server at the University of Michigan and the history database at the University of Kansas. To access the geography server, type the URL: **telnet://martini.eecs.umich.edu3000** in the location box of the browser. Once at this site, the user can find information simply by typing the name of any U.S. city or zip code; the database will display the location's area code, latitude, longitude, population, time zone, elevation, and local features.

The URL for the history database is **telnet://ukanaix.cc.ukans.edu**. The login is "history." From this database, the teacher and student can pull historical information for just about any country or major city. The user simply selects the location, and the database searches for the historical profile.

Another important use of telnet is for users to access their home computer when they are traveling. Suppose a teacher is at a conference and wishes to check his or her e-mail messages. If there is an Internet computer at the conference location, the teacher types his or her home computer's URL using the telnet protocol. Once the home computer is reached, the teacher can use the remote terminal as if it were the home computer. By typing in the login and password, the teacher can access the mail program, read and send e-mail, and perform almost any function that he or she normally can do at home.

File Transfer Protocol

The file transfer protocol, or FTP, is the set of rules that enables users of the Internet to transfer files of information from one computer to another. In education, FTP often is used to copy data files located on a distant host computer to a local computer's hard drive or a floppy disk. Examples of the numerous files of information that may be copied include pictures and descriptions of exhibits located at the Smithsonian Institution, song lyrics, John F. Kennedy's inaugural address, and pictures of musical instruments. Files can be found of almost anything imaginable. After the file is transferred to the local computer, it can be accessed by using a word processor for a text file, a graphics program for a picture, or a multimedia program for a video clip.

Here's how to access an FTP site: First, open the Internet browser, click the "Open" button on the tool bar, and type the URL of the location. To access the Smithsonian Institution, for example, type **ftp://photo1.si.edu** in the location box. The login at most FTP sites is "anonymous," since the host computer does not require the user to establish an account to access the files. This procedure is so common that FTP often is designated as "anonymous." Passwords to enter FTP locations are usually optional; however, it is considered proper Internet etiquette for the user to type his or her e-mail address instead of leaving the line blank.

Next, the user browses the files located at the site and decides which files to copy to the host computer. At the Smithsonian host computer, the files of most interest are located in the **/pub/** or public directory. The directories and files are listed in menu form, similar to a gopher menu. Navigate through the FTP site by highlighting the directories and files, using the arrow and return keys or clicking the mouse. In addition to the file name, the menu often lists the date the file was placed on the server and the size of the file. To copy a file to the local computer, highlight the file name and click the icon that is labeled "get file" or "download now"; the FTP protocol will execute the command. Downloading a file may take several minutes, depending on the size of the file and the speed of the data line. After downloading the desired files, exit the Internet and open the files using local applications.

Important note: All downloaded files should be scanned for viruses. Most schools have experienced problems with a computer that becomes infected with a computer *virus*. With the Internet, instead of just worrying about a virus on the student's disks, educators have to be concerned about viruses in files from around the globe. Every school should have a policy on how to screen for viruses when files are downloaded. A simple procedure is for each computer to have a virus protection program that automatically screens each file for viruses as it is copied onto the hard drive. When a virus is detected, the protection program can then "clean" the file and eliminate the virus.

Newsgroups

Newsgroups, also known as Usenet groups, are the bulletin boards of cyberspace. In most schools, there is a bulletin board for each discipline or subject. Information about the subject-related topics is posted, and students or teachers who walk by read the messages. In similar fashion, users of the Internet may access — or "walk by" — more than 14,000 newsgroups on a myriad of topics. Usenet topics include just about anything imaginable — and some categories that are difficult even to imagine. Most of the newsgroups that are of interest to educators are in the "k12" category. An example would be the newsgroup named **k12.ed.math**. In this newsgroup, secondary school mathematics teachers discuss issues of concern to them. Other newsgroups in the "k12" category include teachers discussing their discipline, students discussing teachers, and students from around the globe working together on projects.

These and the other cyberspace bulletin boards are stored on computers called news servers. To access a newsgroup, one uses a newsgroup program called a newsreader. The newsreader connects the local computer to the news server and the desired newsgroup. When a student or teacher makes the connection, he or she can read the posted messages and then respond to the other users' comments by writing and posting a new message.

Newsgroups can seem rather wild, as anyone with a news server connection may post a message and most newsgroups are not moderated. Thus some postings may be irrelevant to the topic, unorganized, or offensive, even though Usenet etiquette stipulates that messages should be brief, about the newsgroup topic, positive, and pleasant. Another etiquette note, and it applies to all communications on the Internet: Use capital letters only where required; typing in all capital letters is seen as the equivalent of shouting.

Most Internet browsers provide access to newsgroups. For example, with the Netscape browser, choose the "News" command in the Window menu or click the newsgroups directory button to access the "Newsgroup" window. This window contains its own toolbar and menu items for reading, writing, sending, and storing messages. To view all the newsgroup categories, use the mouse to highlight the "Show All Newsgroups" command in the Options menu. A menu of folder icons labeled with the names of newsgroup categories will be displayed in the news window. To view the names of all newsgroups in the "k12" category, as an example, simply click the folder with "k12" as part of the label. That folder will open and display a list of all newsgroups in that category.

If a secondary science teacher scans the list of "k12" newsgroups and is interested in the **k12.ed.news** and **k12.ed.science** newsgroups, he or she may choose to subscribe, or become a regular user of the group, instead of having to find the desired newsgroup in the list of all newsgroups every time. The teacher may subscribe to one or more newsgroups by clicking the "Subscribe" icon next to the newsgroup's name. After clicking the Subscribe icon, the user enters the Options menu and highlights the command to "Show Subscribed Newsgroups." The names of the subscribed newsgroups are stored in a News file, so that they will be displayed whenever the News window is activated. Clicking the name of a newsgroup will access a menu of message headings in

40

that newsgroup, and clicking the message heading will display the contents of the message.

Commands on the News toolbar and the News menu help the user navigate through the newsgroups and respond to posted messages. Basic toolbar commands include "To: News," "Previous," "Next," "Print," and "Stop." The "To: News" button opens a window for writing and posting a message to the newsgroup. Clicking the "Previous" or "Next" button will prompt the browser to access the previous or next message in the newsgroup. When "Print" is clicked, the current message is printed. And clicking "Stop" cancels the transmission of data. These and other commands also are located in the News menu. Many are similar to those found in a word-processing program. Most of the commands are self-explanatory; but if a user gets stuck, help can be found, appropriately, by using the Help menu.

Mailing Lists

Mailing lists are similar to newsgroups except that the messages are delivered to each user's electronic mailbox. Instead of having to access an electronic bulletin board to read and post information, mailing list messages are sent and received using e-mail. This is accomplished using computers housing multiple-destination mailing lists, known as *listservs*. Listserv computers administer mailing lists by receiving, sorting, and distributing messages about a particular topic. Individuals may subscribe to one or many mailing lists. When a mail message is sent to the listserv, it is received by all other subscribers of the mailing list. Users may then reply to received messages by sending a response to all subscribers or only to the person writing the original message. As with newsgroups, many mailing lists are not moderated, and so some of the posted messages may not be deemed appropriate.

Subscribing to a listserv is as simple as sending an e-mail message. Here's how: Open the electronic mail program, type the

Internet address of the listserv in the "To" box, leave the "Subject" box blank, and in the "Text" box type, "subscribe [list name] [person's name]," inserting the name of the desired listserv and the subscriber's name. For example, an educator named Mary Smith who desires to subscribe to the "CURRICUL" mailing list would type in the "To" box: **listserv@saturn.rowan.edu**. She would then type in the "Text" box: **subscribe CURRICUL Mary Smith** and send her e-mail message. After a brief time, ranging from two minutes to two days, Mary Smith will receive an e-mail message indicating that she has successfully subscribed to the mailing list, telling her how to post messages, and also telling her how to "unsubscribe" if she no longer desires the service. (It is wise to print and save this confirmation for future reference.)

Mary Smith notices that she is now receiving e-mail about curriculum and instruction at the K-12 and college levels from the listserv. To become a part of the discussion, all Mary has to do is send an e-mail message stating her opinions. At this point, sending the e-mail to the correct address is critical. The "listserv@domain name" address is used only to subscribe and unsubscribe to the mailing list. Another address is used as the mailing list address. This address is provided with the e-mail message confirming the mailing list subscription and is used to post messages to all other subscribers. At times, a subscriber may want to send a reply only to the person posting a message and not to the whole group. In these instances, the address in the "To" box must be the personal e-mail address of the sender, not the mailing list. All mail sent to the mailing list is forwarded to *all* subscribers. If a subscriber wants to be deleted from the mailing list, a message to "unsubscribe" is sent to the address that was originally used to subscribe to the mailing list.

Accessing Additional Search Engines

In Chapter 2, I discussed procedures for finding needed resources using World Wide Web search tools. Similar search tools are available on the Internet to find FTP and telnet resources, newsgroups, and mailing lists. The server at San Diego State University provides a World Wide Web page that indexes Internet search sites by the type of function or protocol they search and provides hypertext links to those sites. This index site is located at **http://libweb.sdsu.edu/gov/search.html**.

From this page users can link to a desired search engine and find the resources they need. I recommend the following search engines for searching telnet locations:

Hytelnet
http://library.usask.ca/hytelnet

Galaxy
http://galaxy.einet.net/

webCATS
http://library.usask.ca/hywebcat

These search engines provide a guide to library catalogues and other resources that are available using the telnet protocol. After exploring these and other options, the preferred site(s) may be bookmarked for easy future access.

The program that searches for FTP resources is Archie. (Readers may recall that the search engine for Gopher sites is called Veronica, which may strike comic book readers as humorous.) Archie applies the keywords that the user selects, searches the FTP sites, and reports the location of files with information about the requested topic. World Wide Web gateways to Archie searches are at the following URLs:

http://www.lerc.nasa.gov/archieplex/
http://hoohoo.ncsa.uiuc.edu/archie.html

From these web sites, the user will be able to link to Archie and execute the FTP search.

One of the sites for searching Usenet newsgroups is the Alta Vista search engine, which was described Chapter 2. Users can access the Alta Vista site by using: **http://altavista.digital.com/**. When this URL is entered, notice the sentence above the keyword box, "Search the Web and Display the Results in Standard Form." Use the mouse to move the arrow over "the Web" and press the mouse key. The word "Usenet" will appear. Highlight "Usenet" and release the mouse key. The program will now search for newsgroups based on the keywords.

Another search site for newsgroups is Tile Net. This site claims to be a complete reference for Usenet newsgroups. Its URL is **http://tile.net/news/**. Tile Net also provides a reference list to the Internet discussion groups. That URL is **http://tile.net/lists/**.

Finally, yet another database directory for e-mail and discussion groups is Liszt at **http://www.liszt.com/**. To obtain a mailing list directory using only the e-mail function, send the message, "list global," to **listserv@bitnic.educom.com**. A list of mailing lists will be sent by return e-mail. Once the appropriate mailing list is found, subscribe to the listserv using the e-mail function.

CHAPTER FIVE

Road Maps to Curriculum Integration

Computer-based technology and Internet resources are rapidly becoming regular parts of effective instruction at all levels. By using the Internet, educators are providing their students with extensive and diverse resources that enrich and extend the standard curriculum. Teachers who know how to travel the information highway are not bound by obsolete textbooks and other limited or dated classroom materials. They can find the most current information on many subjects and in many forms, such as articles, maps, pictures, sounds, and video clips. By integrating such information with the standard curriculum, teachers can better teach and students can gain more options for learning. Thus the information highway can be a road to greater learning.

Student involvement and learning go beyond the classroom door when Internet resources are incorporated into the curriculum. Most textbooks and other school curriculum materials are written for the so-called average student. When students use the worldwide resources of the Internet to examine content areas, learning becomes individualized and abundant. Not only can information be found for a range of abilities, but students also can explore various facets of a topic according to their interests. And by using the electronic mail feature of the Internet, students can communicate their learning experiences to other students located throughout the school, the school district, the state, and even the world. Classroom projects that once were conducted only in a single classroom or with the classroom across the hall now can be undertaken across borders and oceans.

The Internet as a Resource Tool

Using the Internet as a resource tool is analogous to shopping at the local mall. When we need an item, we visit the store where we are most likely to find that item, hunt through the aisles until we can lay hands on it, and take it up to the cash register. However, not all purchases are planned. Sometimes we just like to wander the mall and browse. If something interesting comes to hand, we may buy it — or we may just file away the information for another day. For educators, the Internet is like an enormous shopping mall stocked to overflowing with interesting and potentially useful curriculum resources. Many of the resources can be sought out specifically, while others can be found by browsing in various interesting sites.

When teachers develop lesson plans, they often require resources that will strengthen the lesson and increase student understanding. Often these resources are not available locally, and so the lesson is taught without them. Now that the Information Age has arrived, instead of doing without the needed materials, teachers can search the Internet and find sites that hold that information. For example, a teacher presenting a science unit on astronomy might want photographs of the planets, but the text does not contain such photographs. Instead of heading for the local library or bookstore to search for the photos, the teacher can sit down at a computer and search the Internet. Using one of the search engines that I described previously, the teacher will come up with several possibilities in a matter of a few minutes. Two of these sites are **http://seds.lpl.arizona.edu/nineplanets/nineplanets/nineplanets.html** and **http://www.nasa.gov**, both of which feature color pictures of the planets. If the teacher has access to a color printer, the pictures can be printed out and handed to students or displayed on the classroom bulletin board. Moreover, students who are interested in knowing more about the planets can visit these same Internet sites on their own, or the entire class can take a "virtual field trip" together by using a projection monitor or gathering around a computer screen under the teacher's supervision.

By browsing these sites, the teacher also may find some other information that can enhance the unit on planets. For example, the NASA site provides a description and pictures of the major moons of the solar system that were taken from NASA spacecraft. The teacher can print these pictures and tie together that information and the information about the planets.

The analogy of the Internet shopping mall is limited if one thinks only of the local mall. The Internet is a global mall — both in terms of international scope and diverse topics. For example, in addition to information that can be integrated into the curriculum, the Internet offers lesson plans, student projects, and online discussion groups. A case in point: At the AskERIC Virtual Library, **http://ericir.syr.edu**, teachers will find lesson plans that have been developed by the Discovery Network, CNN Newsroom, and AskERIC. The AskERIC lesson plans and teaching unit databases are searchable according to topic. Many of the lesson plans include hands-on assignments, experiments, and online activities.

Other sites that provide resources for curriculum planning include the BBN National School Network, the Yanoff List, and Armadillo's K-12 WWW Resources. The BBN National School

Network, **http://copernicus.bbn.com**, and the Yanoff List, **http://www.uwm.edu/mirror/inet.services.html,** will link teachers to lesson plans for the various disciplines, databases listing state and federal curriculum resources, and online student projects. Armadillo's K-12 WWW Resources, **http://chico.rice.edu/armadillo/rice/k12resources.html,** is an index of resources that are arranged by discipline. This web page also has hypertext links to online field trips, museums, and libraries.

Student Projects Using the Internet

It is essential that all students become literate in the use of the Internet and other computer-based technologies. Today's students soon will find themselves in an adult society in which the computer will be used more often than the voice telephone. Already, people can sit at their home computer and, connected to the outside world through a telephone modem, do their banking, pay their bills, analyze the stock market, buy products, and submit their tax returns. Computer-based technologies are involved in almost every occupation and have become one of the most powerful forces in molding the character — and commerce — of late 20th century society.

One of the most positive features of the Internet is its potential for connecting students around the globe. When students from one country work on projects with students from other countries, they develop greater global awareness, which, in turn, prepares them to live and work in the globally interconnected world of the 21st century. They learn to understand and respect people from other cultures, and they explore new choices and examine new responsibilities in a world that is both larger and smaller at the same time.

An example of a popular Internet project is to publish a bilingual newspaper. In one project, three Spanish classes at different schools in the United States linked with students studying English at schools in Spanish-speaking countries. The students wrote, edited, and shared articles using the Internet. The articles covered a variety of topics, including places of interest in the students' areas, favorite foods, local festivals, weather patterns, and politics. Students in each class wrote articles in both their first and second languages. In a short time, the students became more aware of cultural similarities and differences from reading the shared articles.

Opportunities for students to participate in online projects can be found throughout the Internet. A worthwhile site for secondary school science teachers who desire to integrate interactive projects into their curriculum is the NASA K-12 Internet Initiative: Online Interactive Projects. Located at **http://quest.arc.nasa.gov/interactive/index.html**, this site presents interactive projects relating to astronomy, space exploration, and life-in-space research. Projects have included meeting the women of NASA, following NASA's Mars Pathfinder, and visiting with researchers in Antarctica over the Internet.

Another web site of interest to all teachers who use technology in the classroom is the home page for Wentworth Worldwide Media, the publisher of the newsletter, *Classroom Connect*. The home page, **http://www.wentworth.com/wentworth**, contains articles from *Classroom Connect* and links to other educational sites. This newsletter is a practical guide to the Internet that is written in easy-to-understand language. The articles provide information about lesson plans, global projects, news about the Internet, and other helpful information.

Yet another place to find or propose online interactive projects is in the education or "k12" newsgroups. For example, a social studies teacher accessing the **k12.ed.soc-studies** newsgroup often can find postings by teachers proposing interactive online projects. One recent posting suggested that students from different classrooms research the topic of welfare and present their ideas and beliefs in a journal. The message included the e-mail address of the educator who wrote the original message. Teachers who were interested in having their class be part of the project e-mailed the teacher and had their students submit, edit, and evaluate articles. The journal was published on the Internet and in hard copy form at the participating schools.

When an appropriate project for their class cannot be found in a newsgroup, teachers may post their own suggestions. Teachers new to Internet work might want to take up the challenge to design a project that would be useful and of interest to their class (and other classes) and then present the proposal in the newsgroup. Newcomers to this activity may be concerned that few other readers may be interested; however, the opposite usually is true. Instead of getting too few responses, the posting teacher often receives more replies than expected. The teachers e-mail each other, finalize the project, and incorporate it into the curriculum.

Evaluating Internet Resources

As in the case of any resource, both verification and evaluation are essential. Teachers should evaluate information obtained on the Internet before incorporating it into the curriculum. Many educators spend a considerable amount of time evaluating textbooks, journal articles, and other sources of knowledge before deciding what materials to use in the classroom. Using Internet resources requires teachers to perform the same type of evaluation procedures they use when examining the more traditional sources of information. Teachers understand that just because data is in print does not make it true, accurate, or valid. Similarly, information is not true, accurate, valid, or useful just because it is found on the Internet. This fact may be especially true of Internet resources, because almost anyone with Internet access can post information to the network without any peer-evaluation process.

A strategic step when evaluating Internet information is to establish its location. This information often can be determined by the domain name and the top-domain name in the site's URL. For example, a teacher searching for information about Supreme Court decisions would find information at **http://www.law.cornell.edu/lii.table.html**. The top-domain "edu" signifies an education institution and the domain name "cornell" indicates that the file server with the information is provided by Cornell University. If the domain name does not readily signify the site, the location often is part of the location's home page information. Most educators, on reading the URL, **http://sln.fi.edu**, would know only that the file server was located at an education institution or organization. When the home page is accessed, the page title indicates that "fi" stands for Franklin Institute. Information located at prominent education institutions or organizations, such as Cornell University and the Franklin Institute, usually is well-managed and accurate.

Government locations are another reliable source for curriculum information. Educators who desire information and details about the executive branch of the United State's government may access the White House at **http://www.whitehouse.gov**. The top-domain "gov" indicates government, and the domain name "whitehouse" indicates who provides the information. Educators are well advised to check the top-domain name in every case. There was (perhaps still is) a page on the World Wide Web with the address "www.whitehouse.org" that was a parody of the official White House location. The "org," for those in the know, is the giveaway.

Sites with the top-domain name "org," for organization, or "com," for commercial, should be evaluated closely. Many "org" and "com" locations have useful information, while others present meaningless drivel. With these top-domain names, teachers must identify the providing organization. For example, teachers who access the URL **http://www.aas.org** soon discover that "aas" is the American Astronomical Society, a major professional organization in North America for astronomers. Thus they will assign more credence to the information provided in this site than if the organization was not well known.

Educators should be even more careful regarding information received from mailing lists or posted to newsgroups. Most mailing lists and newsgroups are not moderated, and messages are not reviewed before they are distributed. Because anyone with Internet access can write and post a message, information may be inaccurate, illogical, and, in some cases, deranged. This is not to say that useful information cannot be found in these areas but simply that it should be evaluated carefully for accuracy.

Another part of the evaluation process is to compare information found on the Internet with information located in other sources. Because the Internet is only one of many resource tools available to teachers and students, teachers and students alike can verify information obtained using the Internet with data found in textbooks, journal and magazine articles, newspapers, and other sources. Good education demands adherence to the maxim: Do not rely on only one source. For example, a chemistry class accessed a hypertext version of the periodic table at **http://www.cchem.berkeley.edu/table/index.html**. The table is presented in traditional form; however, when an element is highlighted, detailed information, such as the element's standard state, color, discoverer, and name meaning, is presented. To verify this information, the students compared the table from the Internet to the information in their textbook. They found that information from both sources supports the accuracy of the Internet-based periodic table.

The students also noticed that "berkeley.edu" was the site's domain and top-domain names. These names indicate that the periodic table is provided by the University of California at Berkeley. As Berkeley is a prominent university, the students had even more confidence regarding the accuracy of the data.

Verification and evaluation also can be accomplished using the Internet itself. Most sites on the Internet are independent, and so information at one site may be compared with information at another site. An example would be to compare data about the solar system at the NASA home page, **http://www.nasa.gov**, with information located at **http://seds.lpl.arizona.edu/nineplanets/nineplanets/nineplanets.html**. If the details about the solar system at the two sites are similar, then the information probably is reliable. However, continued evaluation would be required if the details about the solar system did not agree. In this example, a minor discrepancy was noted. On further investigation, it became apparent that the difference in information was the result of one site not being as up-to-date as the other. This problem is understandable, because astronomers constantly are discovering new knowledge. At the time of the student search, one Internet site had updated its file with the new information, but the other was not as quick to update. This brings up another tip: A helpful practice when using the Internet is to check when the file lists were last updated. This procedure is comparable to checking the copyright date of a book or the publication date of a journal article.

When computer-based technologies were first being developed, many pundits and prognosticators said that the computer eventually would replace the teacher. The opposite has happened. Instead of replacing classroom teachers, increasing computer use amplifies the need for competent teachers who can design meaningful learning environments that integrate multiple sources of information. Locating Internet resources, verifying and evaluating them, and incorporating such information into the standard curriculum requires teachers who are computer-literate, computer-competent, and electronically adventurous. Teachers also plan student projects and establish procedures that will help students develop their own computer competence and the requisite higher-order thinking skills to reconcile conflicting information on the Internet.

According to recent research, student learning increases that are attributable to computer technology occur only when a teacher has evaluated the technology and rationally incorporated well-designed, computer-based applications into the curriculum.

Avoiding Inappropriate Material

A growing concern among educators is the availability of "inappropriate" material on the Internet. Depending on definition, inappropriate resources available using the Internet include such things as pornographic pictures, hate speech, and instructions regarding how to build and detonate explosives. These kinds of information are readily available to anyone who has access to the World Wide Web and newsgroups. Often, however, they are found by accident, rather than by intention. In one case, for example, a student performed an Internet search using "Venus" as the keyword. He was attempting to find a picture of the planet Venus. But on his list of possible sites was a topless nightclub that had the word "Venus" in its name. Needless to say, the topless nightclub site probably would not be considered suitable for school use.

Another area where offensive materials are located is in the Usenet newsgroups. I discussed the "k12" newsgroups previously. This category contains newsgroups in which teachers can communicate about different education topics and disciplines. A less "appropriate" category (educationally speaking) might be the "alt.sex" category, which includes newsgroups about almost anything sexually imaginable. There are newsgroups in this category that are well-known for their explicit descriptions and pictures of different sex acts. At one major U.S. university, the administrators limited student access to this category after students collected 97,000 digitally encoded pornographic pictures using the university's computers.

When students access Internet resources at school, they should be engaged in school-related work. Many schools closely monitor student use of the Internet to be certain that the computers are used in an "appropriate" manner, sometimes (but not always) specifically defining what is appropriate. Many schools designate a particular location, such as the media center or a dedicated computer lab, for their student-accessible computers that are connected to the Internet. When the computers are in one location, a designated educator can observe the computer screens and monitor the sites that students are accessing. Individual teachers can help with the monitoring process by carefully defining Internet-related assignments and making sure the computer coordinator knows what the students should be doing at the computer.

Another method used by educators to limit student access to inappropriate sites is to obtain software programs that keep students from accessing certain Internet locations based on the content of the site or the site's URL. To activate the software, the person responsible for maintaining the school computer network loads the program and sets the appropriate restrictions. One restriction used by many educators is to deny student access to any newsgroup with the word "sex" in its name. If students attempt to access a site deemed unsuitable, the computer screen simply displays a message that the location cannot be accessed.

However, regardless of how thorough educators are in trying to limit access to inappropriate sites, some students will be able to slip past the censors. If major companies and organizations cannot prevent unauthorized access of their computers, it is highly unlikely that the local school will be successful at preventing all student access to forbidden sites. Thus the following advice has been put forth by a number of computer authorities: Each school should develop clear policies regarding student use of the Internet and the consequences for violating such policies. Many schools now ask their students (and parents) to agree to the policy statement and sign it before allowing the students to use the Internet.

***

The Internet, like all other aspects of our Information Age society, has positives and negatives. But schools must prepare today's students for the technological environment that they will encounter as adults in the 21st century. The Internet will be a major part of that world. In all likelihood, people who do not know how to use technology will be as lost in tomorrow's world as people who do not read are left behind today. Educators must continually assess the pluses and minuses of our ever-changing technological landscape. A road is only as good as the destination to which it leads. Only by understanding computer technology will students be able to control it, integrate it into their lives, and use it humanely. The information highway offers an exciting road to the future.

GLOSSARY

browser: A communication program that enables the Internet user to search for World Wide Web resources.

default: In computer parlance, the document or operation that a computer is programmed to display or perform unless the user specifies otherwise.

domain name: The part of an Internet address located after the @ sign that indicates the name of the host computer. See also, **top-domain name**.

e-mail: Written messages, to which other files may be attached, that are electronically transmitted over a computer network.

file transfer protocol: Usually written as FTP, one method by which files may be transferred from one computer to another.

Gopher: An Internet program that enables users to access information housed on a particular type of server program; now largely supplanted by the World Wide Web (hypertext).

hard copy: Text or other information printed on paper.

home page: The first document displayed when a user accesses a site on the Internet.

host: A computer with direct access to the Internet that serves as a connection point for networked users. Example: America Online is a major Internet provider, or host.

http: Abbreviation of "Hypertext Transfer Protocol"; used to specify the method to be used to locate documents on the Internet.

hypermedia: A computer-based information retrieval system whereby users can view (and in most cases download) text, audio and video recordings, still photographs, and graphic images, such as maps and charts.

hypertext: Text that contains "links," shown as highlighted words, to other documents. The highlighted words can be clicked to retrieve the linked document without typing in the URL address.

icon: A small graphic or picture that visually represents a function. Example: a disk used to symbolize the "save" function.

keyword: A word or group of words used to define a search of Internet resources.

listserv: A computer program dedicated to managing mailing lists for electronic mail groups.

login: Used as a noun or a verb. An account name (noun); the act of entering a computer system (verb). Account names are not secret or secure. See also, **password**.

modem: Short for "modulator/demodulator." A device that allows computers to be connected by means of telephone lines.

network: A number of computers that are electronically connected to one another.

newsgroup: The name given to discussion groups on the Internet.

password: A unique combination of letters and numbers that prevents someone else from using the same account.

search engine: A computer program the enables the user to locate Internet information by using keywords.

telnet: A protocol that allows users to log onto a computer from a remote location.

top-domain name: The part of an Internet address located after the domain name that indicates the type of location, such as "org" for organization. See also, **domain name**.

Usenet: Short for "user's network." See, **newsgroup**.

username: The part of an Internet address before the @ sign that indicates the identity of the person or organization with an Internet account on the host computer.

virus: A coding error that can cause computer programs to malfunction, or "crash," and that can be transferred from one computer to another by file transfer.